BLAZERS

LINE OF DUTY

CRIME SCENE INVESTIGATORS

UNCOVERING THE TRUTH

by Connie Colwell Miller

Reading Consultant
Barbara J. Fox
Reading Specialist
North Carolina State University

Content Consultant
David Foran, PhD
Director, Forensic Science Program
Michigan State University

Capstone press

Mankato, Minnesota

Blazers is published by Capstone Press,
151 Good Counsel Drive, P.O. Box 669, Mankato, Minnesota 56002.
www.capstonepress.com

Library of Congress Cataloging-in-Publication Data
Miller, Connie Colwell, 1976–
    Crime scene investigators: uncovering the truth / by Connie Colwell Miller.
    p. cm. — (Blazers. Line of duty)
    Summary: "Describes crime scene investigators, including what they do and
how they help catch criminals" — Provided by publisher.
    Includes bibliographical references and index.
    ISBN–13: 978-1-4296-1272-2 (hardcover)
    ISBN–10: 1-4296-1272-X (hardcover)
    1. Criminal investigation — Juvenile literature. 2. Crime scene searches —
Juvenile literature. I. Title. II. Series.
HV8073.8.M55 2008
363.25'2 — dc22   *I 656 73 I*   2007024827

Editorial Credits
Aaron Sautter, editor; Bobbi J. Wyss, designer; Wanda Winch, photo researcher

1 2 3 4 5 6 13 12 11 10 09 08

TABLE OF CONTENTS

ON THE SCENE

A dead body is found on the sidewalk. No one knows what happened. Crime scene **investigators** (CSIs) are called in to look for clues.

[**investigator** — someone who studies crime scenes]

A CSI unit studies a stolen car. They look for **fingerprints** and other clues. They find a gun hidden in the trunk.

[**fingerprint** — the pattern made by the tips of your fingers]

A CSI unit is called to a bank. Someone has broken into the bank's safe. A CSI dusts for fingerprints.

GATHERING EVIDENCE

CSI units are part of many police forces. CSIs work with detectives and other police officers to collect clues.

CSI units take lots of pictures. They need to record the scene exactly as it is. Moving anything could ruin an important clue.

 CSIs sometimes take photos of wounds on injured victims.

CSIs dust crime scenes for fingerprints. They use tape to lift fingerprints off a surface. Then they put the tape on a fingerprint card.

CSIs look for blood at crime scenes. They use bright lights or special chemicals to find bloodstains. They put blood samples in paper bags.

FACT! CSIs use a chemical called luminol to make bloodstains glow in the dark.

CSI members look for bullets. They look for bullet holes too. The holes can help them learn where the shooter was located.

THE CRIME LAB

CSI units take **evidence** to crime labs. Lab workers look for more clues. Markings on a bullet can show which gun was used in a crime.

[**evidence** — information or objects found at a crime scene]

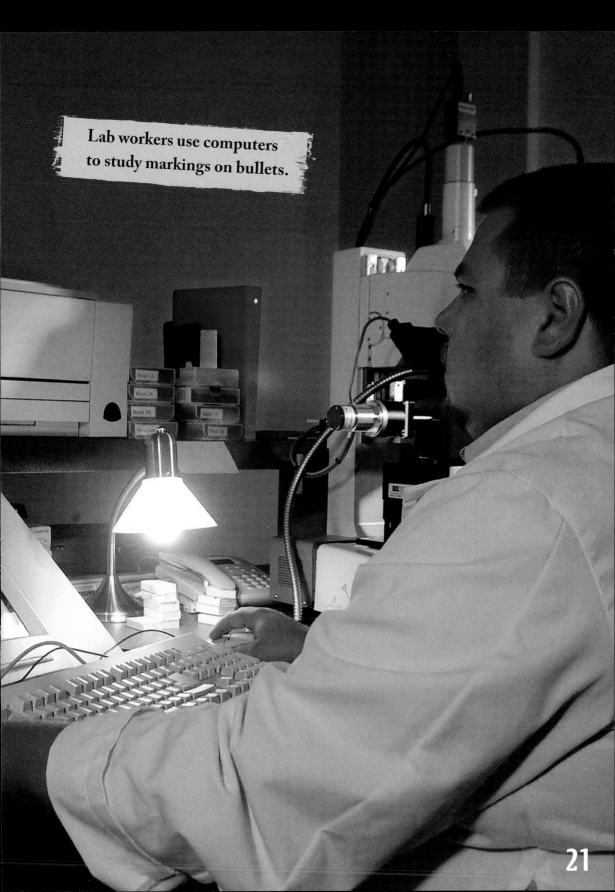

Lab workers use computers to study markings on bullets.

Lab workers use the Automated Fingerprint Identification System (AFIS). This computer system matches fingerprints with known **criminals**.

[**criminal** — someone who commits a crime]

FACT! Smeared fingerprints don't have enough detail to make a match with a known criminal.

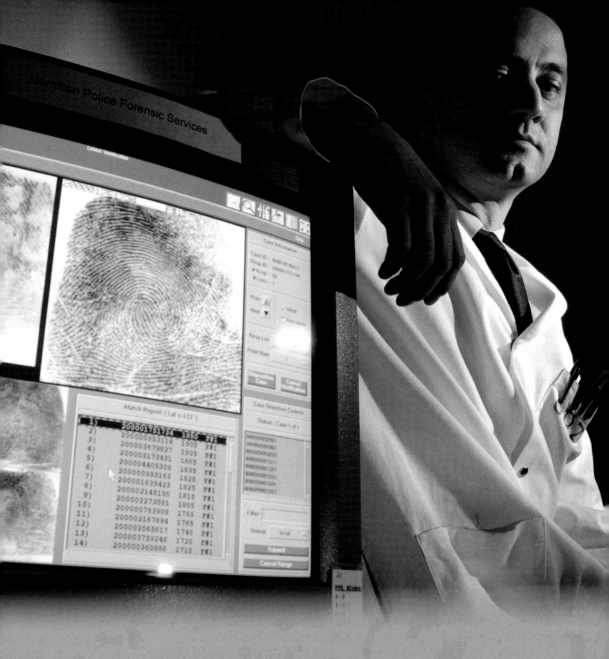

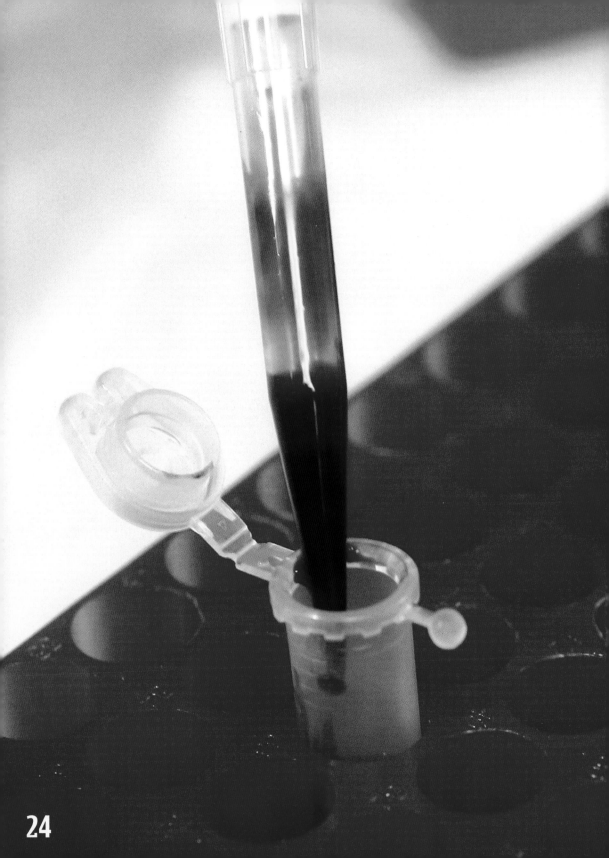

Lab workers test blood samples for **DNA** evidence. DNA is different in every person. It can prove that someone was at a crime scene.

[**DNA** — material in body cells that are unique to each person]

SHARING CLUES

CSI units share clues with police detectives and lawyers. Police use the clues to find and catch **suspects**.

[**suspect** — someone thought to be guilty of a crime]

FACT! CSIs share the clues and information they gather at trials.

27

FACT! CSIs can study bugs on a body to learn how long the person has been dead.

Criminals won't get away when CSIs are on the case. CSI units find the clues that bring criminals to **justice**.

[**justice** — punishment for breaking the law]

29

GLOSSARY

criminal (KRIM-uh-nuhl) — someone who commits a crime

DNA (dee-en-AY) — material in body cells that gives people their unique characteristics

evidence (EV-uh-duhnss) — information or objects that provide proof of who committed a crime

fingerprint (FING-gur-print) — the pattern made by the curved ridges on the tips of your fingers

investigator (in-VESS-tuh-gate-ur) — someone who studies a crime scene to find out how a crime was commited and who did it

justice (JUHSS–tiss) — when punishment is given for breaking the law

lawyer (LAW-yur) — someone who is trained to speak for people in court

suspect (SUHSS-pekt) — a person believed to be responsible for a crime

victim (VIK-tuhm) — a person who is hurt, killed, or suffers because of a crime

READ MORE

Rollins, Barbara B. and Michael Dahl. *Blood Evidence.* Forensic Crime Solvers. Mankato, Minn.: Capstone Press, 2004.

Scott, Carey. *Crime Scene Detective: Become a Forensics Super Sleuth, with Do-It-Yourself Activities.* New York: DK, 2007.

INTERNET SITES

FactHound offers a safe, fun way to find Internet sites related to this book. All of the sites on FactHound have been researched by our staff.

Here's how:
1. Visit *www.facthound.com*
2. Choose your grade level.
3. Type in this special code **142961272X** for age-appropriate sites. You may also browse subjects by clicking on letters, or by clicking on pictures and words.
4. Click on the **Fetch It** button.

FactHound will fetch the best sites for you!

INDEX

4/12   2   7/08
1-16   2   ———
3|17   2   ———
2|21   2   7/08
11|22   2   7/08
7|24   2   7/08